Table of Contents

Introduction

Chapter 1: Types of SBA Loans

Chapter 2: Preparing for the SBA Loan Application

Chapter 3: The SBA Loan Application Process

Chapter 4: Writing a Strong Business Plan

Chapter 5: Financial Statements and Projections

Chapter 6: Collateral and Personal Guarantees

Chapter 7: Working with an SBA-Approved Lender

Chapter 8: The SBA Loan Underwriting Process

Chapter 9: Closing the Loan

Chapter 10: Managing Your SBA Loan

Chapter 11: SBA Loan Resources and Assistance

Chapter 12: Common FAQs

Introduction

Welcome to "Navigating the SBA Loan Application Process: A Comprehensive Guide." In the world of small business, access to capital is often a determining factor between success and struggle. Whether you are starting a new venture, expanding your existing business, or recovering from unforeseen setbacks, securing the right funding is critical. This ebook serves as your definitive resource to understanding and navigating the complexities of the Small Business Administration (SBA) loan application process.

Understanding SBA Loans

The Small Business Administration (SBA) is a U.S. government agency that provides support to entrepreneurs and small businesses. One of the key ways it fulfills this mission is through its various loan programs. Unlike conventional loans, SBA loans are partially guaranteed by the government, which significantly reduces the risk for lenders. This guarantee enables lenders to offer more favorable terms and make loans available to small businesses that might not qualify under standard lending criteria.

Types of SBA Loans

The SBA offers a range of loan programs tailored to different business needs:

- **SBA 7(a) Loan Program:** The most common SBA loan, providing financial help for businesses with special requirements.
- **SBA 504 Loan Program:** Offers financing for major fixed assets such as real estate or equipment.
- **SBA Microloans:** Provides small, short-term loans for working capital or the purchase of inventory, supplies, furniture, fixtures, machinery, or equipment.
- **Disaster Loans:** Available to businesses, homeowners, and renters to repair or replace property damaged by a disaster.
- **Export Loans:** Designed to help businesses expand their export activities.

Importance of SBA Loans for Small Businesses

SBA loans play an essential role in the small business ecosystem by providing access to capital that fuels growth, innovation, and sustainability. Here are some key benefits of SBA loans:

1. **Lower Down Payments:** SBA loans often require lower down payments compared to conventional loans, making them more accessible for small business owners.
2. **Extended Repayment Terms:** Longer repayment periods mean lower monthly payments, which can improve cash flow and financial stability.
3. **Competitive Interest Rates:** SBA loans generally offer lower interest rates than traditional loans, reducing the overall cost of borrowing.
4. **Flexibility:** SBA loans can be used for a variety of purposes, including working capital, inventory, equipment purchases, real estate, and debt refinancing.

Overview of the SBA Loan Application Process

The SBA loan application process can be intricate, but understanding each step can make it more manageable. Here's a high-level overview of the process:

1. **Assess Your Needs and Eligibility:** Determine how much funding you need and which type of SBA loan is best suited for your business. Review the eligibility criteria to ensure you qualify.
2. **Gather Documentation:** Prepare all necessary documentation, including your business plan, financial statements, and tax returns. Proper documentation is critical to a successful application.
3. **Choose an SBA-Approved Lender:** Find a lender that participates in SBA loan programs. Building a relationship with your lender can facilitate the application process.
4. **Submit Your Application:** Complete the loan application and submit it along with the required documentation. Accuracy and completeness are crucial at this stage.
5. **Loan Underwriting and Approval:** The lender will review your application and perform underwriting to assess the risk. Be prepared to answer questions and provide additional information.
6. **Loan Closing:** Once approved, you'll go through the closing process, where you'll sign the final loan documents and receive the funds.
7. **Manage Your Loan:** After disbursement, focus on making timely payments and managing your loan terms. If you encounter financial difficulties, seek assistance promptly.

This guide will delve into each of these steps in detail, providing practical tips and insights to help you navigate the SBA loan application process with confidence. Additionally, we will explore common challenges and how to overcome them, ensuring you are well-prepared for every aspect of securing an SBA loan.

By the end of this guide, you will have a thorough understanding of how SBA loans work, how to apply for them, and how to manage them effectively. Our goal is to empower you with the knowledge and tools you need to secure the funding your business requires to thrive.

Chapter 1: Types of SBA Loans

The Small Business Administration (SBA) provides various loan programs to support small businesses in the United States. Understanding the different types of SBA loans is crucial for business owners seeking financing. This chapter will detail each primary SBA loan program, providing clarity on their purposes, eligibility criteria, and application processes.

SBA 7(a) Loan Program

The SBA 7(a) Loan Program is the most common and versatile SBA loan, designed to help small businesses with a wide range of financing needs.

Purpose:

The 7(a) loan can be used for various purposes, including:

- **Working capital**: Funds to cover day-to-day operating expenses.
- **Equipment purchases**: Financing to buy machinery, vehicles, or technology.
- **Real estate acquisition or renovation**: Funds for buying, building, or renovating commercial real estate.
- **Refinancing existing debt**: Consolidating high-interest debts into one lower-interest loan.
- **Purchasing inventory**: Capital to buy products for resale or materials to produce goods.
- **Expanding the business**: Resources for business growth, such as new locations or markets.

Eligibility:

To be eligible for an SBA 7(a) loan, businesses must meet the following criteria:

- **Operate for profit**: Only for-profit businesses qualify.
- **Be considered a small business according to SBA size standards**: Must meet industry-specific size standards based on employee count or annual receipts.
- **Operate in the United States or its territories**: Business location must be within the U.S., Puerto Rico, the U.S. Virgin Islands, or Guam.
- **Demonstrate a need for the loan**: Must show that the loan is necessary and will benefit the business.
- **Use alternative financial resources, including personal assets, before seeking SBA assistance**: Owners must invest their own time and money.

- **Show the ability to repay the loan**: Must have a solid credit history and cash flow to service the debt.

Application Process:

1. **Prepare Your Documents**: Gather necessary financial statements, tax returns, a detailed business plan, and other relevant documents.
   - **Business plan**: Include a detailed description of your business, market analysis, and financial projections.
   - **Financial statements**: Profit and loss statements, balance sheets, and cash flow statements.
   - **Tax returns**: Business and personal tax returns for the past three years.
2. **Choose a Lender**: Find an SBA-approved lender. Many banks and credit unions offer SBA loans.
   - **Research lenders**: Look for lenders with experience in SBA loans and a good reputation.
   - **Interview potential lenders**: Ask about their process, fees, and requirements.
3. **Submit Your Application**: Work with your lender to complete the SBA loan application.
   - **Complete forms**: SBA Form 1919 (Borrower Information Form) and SBA Form 413 (Personal Financial Statement).
   - **Provide additional documentation**: Business licenses, leases, and other relevant documents.
4. **Loan Review**: The lender reviews your application and submits it to the SBA for approval.
   - **Credit check**: The lender will check your personal and business credit scores.
   - **Underwriting**: The lender evaluates your financial health and loan eligibility.
5. **Approval and Disbursement**: Upon approval, the lender disburses the funds to your business.
   - **Loan closing**: Sign the loan agreement and receive the funds.
   - **Use of funds**: Ensure that the loan proceeds are used according to the agreed-upon purposes.

SBA 504 Loan Program

The SBA 504 Loan Program provides long-term, fixed-rate financing for major assets that promote business growth and job creation.

Purpose:

The 504 loan can be used for:

- **Purchasing land or existing buildings**: Acquiring commercial real estate.
- **Constructing new facilities**: Building new offices, warehouses, or production facilities.
- **Modernizing, renovating, or converting existing facilities**: Upgrading or expanding current business premises.
- **Purchasing long-term machinery or equipment**: Buying high-value machinery or equipment with a long useful life.

Eligibility:

Eligibility criteria for the 504 loan include:

- **Tangible net worth of less than $15 million**: Business's tangible net worth must not exceed this limit.
- **Average net income of less than $5 million after federal income taxes for the two years preceding the application**: Ensures the business is genuinely small.
- **The loan must create or retain jobs or meet other public policy goals**: Typically, one job must be created or retained for every $65,000 borrowed.

Application Process:

1. **Work with a CDC**: Certified Development Companies (CDCs) are nonprofit corporations that promote economic development. They work with the SBA and private-sector lenders to provide 504 loans.
    - **Find a CDC**: Locate a CDC in your area through the SBA website.
2. **Prepare Your Documents**: Gather detailed financial information, including a business plan, financial statements, and tax returns.
    - **Detailed project cost breakdown**: Include costs for land, buildings, machinery, and equipment.
    - **Job creation/retention documentation**: Outline how the loan will create or retain jobs.
3. **Submit Your Application**: The CDC helps you prepare and submit the loan application to the SBA.

- o **Complete forms**: SBA Form 1244 (Application for Section 504 Loans) and other required documents.
4. **Approval and Disbursement**: Upon approval, the SBA and the private-sector lender fund the loan.
    - o **Loan structure**: Typically, 50% from a private lender, 40% from the CDC/SBA, and 10% from the borrower.
    - o **Use of funds**: Follow the approved project plan to use the funds.

SBA Microloans

The SBA Microloan Program provides small, short-term loans to small businesses and certain types of not-for-profit childcare centers.

Purpose:

Microloans can be used for:

- **Working capital**: Funds for day-to-day operations.
- **Inventory or supplies**: Purchasing goods or materials.
- **Furniture or fixtures**: Buying office furniture or retail fixtures.
- **Machinery or equipment**: Acquiring small-scale machinery or technology.

Eligibility:

To qualify for a microloan, businesses must:

- **Meet the SBA's size standards**: Must qualify as a small business.
- **Demonstrate the ability to repay the loan**: Show sufficient cash flow and creditworthiness.
- **Work with an SBA-approved intermediary lender**: Loans are provided through nonprofit community-based organizations.

Application Process:

1. **Contact an Intermediary Lender**: These are nonprofit community-based organizations with experience in lending and technical assistance.
    - o **Locate a lender**: Find a list of approved intermediaries on the SBA website.
2. **Prepare Your Documents**: Provide detailed information about your business, including financial statements and a business plan.

- **Business plan**: Include an overview of the business, market strategy, and financial forecasts.
- **Financial statements**: Current profit and loss statements and balance sheets.

3. **Submit Your Application**: Work with the intermediary lender to complete and submit your application.
    - **Complete forms**: Intermediary-specific application forms and supporting documents.
4. **Approval and Disbursement**: The intermediary lender reviews your application and disburses the funds upon approval.
    - **Loan terms**: Typically, microloans range from $500 to $50,000 with a maximum term of six years.
    - **Use of funds**: Ensure proper use of the microloan according to the business plan.

SBA Disaster Loans

The SBA Disaster Loan Program provides low-interest loans to businesses, homeowners, and renters affected by declared disasters.

Purpose:

Disaster loans can be used for:

- **Repairing or replacing real estate, personal property, machinery, equipment, inventory, and business assets damaged or destroyed in a declared disaster**: Covering the costs of recovery and rebuilding.

Eligibility:

Eligibility criteria include:

- **Being located in a declared disaster area**: Must be within the designated disaster zone.
- **Demonstrating the ability to repay the loan**: Must have the financial capacity to repay.
- **Providing collateral for loans over $25,000**: Securing the loan with assets if the amount exceeds this threshold.

Application Process:

1. **Apply Online or in Person**: Applications can be submitted online through the SBA's Disaster Loan Assistance portal or in person at a Disaster Recovery Center.
    - **Visit Disaster Recovery Centers**: Centers provide in-person assistance with applications.

2. **Prepare Your Documents**: Gather information about your business or property, including financial statements and estimates of damage.
    - **Damage assessment**: Provide detailed descriptions and photographs of the damage.
    - **Repair estimates**: Include quotes from contractors or repair services.
3. **Submit Your Application**: Complete and submit the application to the SBA.
    - **Complete forms**: SBA Form 5 (Business Loan Application) or SBA Form 5C (Home Loan Application) and other required documents.
4. **Inspection and Approval**: The SBA conducts an inspection of the damaged property and reviews the application. Upon approval, the SBA disburses the funds.
    - **Loan terms**: Low-interest rates with long repayment terms, typically up to 30 years.
    - **Use of funds**: Ensure funds are used for repair and replacement purposes as approved.

SBA Export Loans

The SBA Export Loan Programs are designed to help small businesses expand or develop export activities.

Purpose:

Export loans can be used for:

- **Financing export orders**: Providing working capital to fulfill export sales.
- **Improving export working capital**: Supporting operations involved in exporting.
- **Enhancing international trade operations**: Investing in international marketing, trade shows, and foreign distribution.

Types of Export Loans:

1. **Export Express Loan Program**: Provides loans up to $500,000 for businesses looking to expand their export activities.
    - **Fast approval**: Typically, a 36-hour turnaround time for loan decisions.
    - **Flexible use of funds**: Can be used for various export-related expenses.
2. **Export Working Capital Program (EWCP)**: Provides working capital to support export sales, with loan amounts up to $5 million.

- **Revolving lines of credit**: Offers short-term working capital for export transactions.
- **Guarantees**: SBA guarantees up to 90% of the loan amount.

3. **International Trade Loan Program**: Offers loans up to $5 million to support export transactions, refinance debt, and improve export competitiveness.
    - **Long-term financing**: Can be used for fixed assets or working capital related to international trade.
    - **Debt refinancing**: Allows refinancing of existing debt to improve financial stability.

Eligibility:

Eligibility criteria vary by loan type but generally include:

- **Being in business for at least 12 months**: Ensuring the business is established.
- **Demonstrating the ability to generate export sales**: Showing a track record of export activities or potential.

Application Process:

1. **Contact an SBA-Approved Lender**: Find a lender experienced in SBA export loan programs.
    - **Locate lenders**: Use the SBA website or local SBA office to find qualified lenders.
2. **Prepare Your Documents**: Gather financial statements, business plans, and export-related documentation.
    - **Export business plan**: Include details on international market strategy and potential sales.
    - **Financial statements**: Recent profit and loss statements, balance sheets, and cash flow projections.
3. **Submit Your Application**: Work with the lender to complete and submit the application.
    - **Complete forms**: SBA Form 1920 (Lender's Application for Guaranty) and other relevant documents.
4. **Approval and Disbursement**: The lender reviews the application and submits it to the SBA for approval. Upon approval, funds are disbursed to support export activities.
    - **Loan terms**: Vary depending on the type of export loan and lender policies.

- **Use of funds**: Ensure proper use of loan proceeds for export-related expenses.

By understanding the different types of SBA loans, business owners can make informed decisions about which loan program best suits their needs. Each loan type has specific purposes, eligibility criteria, and application processes, ensuring that small businesses have access to the financing they need to thrive.

Chapter 2: Preparing for the SBA Loan Application

Assessing Your Business Needs

Before applying for an SBA loan, it's crucial to conduct a thorough assessment of your business needs. This process will help you determine how the loan can best support your business goals and ensure that you are requesting an appropriate amount of funding. Here's a step-by-step guide to assessing your business needs:

1. **Identifying the Purpose of the Loan:**
   - Expansion: Are you looking to expand your business, such as opening a new location, increasing production capacity, or entering new markets? Outline the specific expansion goals and how the loan will help achieve them.
   - Equipment Purchase: Do you need new machinery or technology to improve efficiency or production quality? List the equipment required, its cost, and how it will enhance your business operations.
   - Working Capital: Is the loan intended to cover day-to-day operational expenses, such as payroll, inventory, or rent? Detail your monthly operating costs and how the loan will help manage cash flow.
   - Debt Refinancing: Are you seeking to refinance existing high-interest debt to improve cash flow? Calculate the total debt to be refinanced and the interest savings expected from the SBA loan.
   - Other Purposes: Specify any other reasons for seeking the loan, such as research and development, marketing campaigns, or emergency funds.

2. **Determining the Amount of Funding:**
   - Detailed Budgeting: Create a detailed budget that includes all anticipated expenses related to the loan's purpose. This should include quotes from suppliers, cost estimates, and any other financial projections.
   - Contingency Planning: Include a contingency amount to cover unexpected costs. This ensures you have sufficient funds even if costs exceed initial estimates.
   - Professional Assistance: Consider consulting with a financial advisor or accountant to validate your funding requirements and ensure your budget is realistic and comprehensive.

3. **Evaluating Repayment Ability:**
   - Cash Flow Analysis: Conduct a thorough analysis of your business's cash flow to ensure you can manage the additional debt. This includes examining historical

cash flow statements and projecting future cash flows with the loan payments included.
- Debt Service Coverage Ratio (DSCR): Calculate your DSCR, which is your net operating income divided by your total debt service. A DSCR of 1.25 or higher is typically considered healthy and indicates that you can comfortably cover loan payments.
- Scenario Planning: Prepare different financial scenarios (best-case, worst-case, and most likely) to understand how various conditions might impact your ability to repay the loan.

Understanding Eligibility Requirements

Each SBA loan program has specific eligibility criteria that must be met. Understanding these requirements will help you determine if your business qualifies and guide you in preparing your application.

1. **Business Type and Location:**
    - For-Profit Status: Your business must operate for profit. Non-profit organizations are generally not eligible for SBA loans.
    - U.S. Operations: Your business must be physically located and operate in the United States or its territories. This includes having a U.S.-based headquarters and conducting primary business activities within the country.

2. **Size Standards:**
    - Industry-Specific Criteria: SBA size standards vary by industry, typically based on the number of employees or annual revenue. For example, a manufacturing business might qualify as small if it has fewer than 500 employees, while a retail business might qualify with less than $7.5 million in annual receipts.
    - Check Size Standards: Use the SBA's size standards tool available on their website to determine if your business meets the criteria for your specific industry.

3. **Equity Investment:**
    - Owner's Investment: The SBA requires business owners to have invested their own time and money into the business. This equity investment demonstrates your commitment and reduces the lender's risk.
    - Documentation of Investment: Provide evidence of your equity investment, such as bank statements, receipts, or financial records showing the capital you have invested in the business.

4. **Need for the Loan:**
    - Lack of Alternative Financing: Demonstrate that you have explored other financing options and that an SBA loan is necessary to meet your business needs. This might include letters of denial from other lenders or a narrative explaining why traditional financing is not sufficient.
    - Detailed Explanation: Prepare a detailed explanation of why the loan is needed and how it will be used to achieve specific business goals. This should align with the purpose and amount of funding determined earlier.

Gathering Necessary Documentation

Having the required documentation ready can significantly streamline the SBA loan application process and improve your chances of approval. Here's a comprehensive list of documents you'll need:

1. **Business Plan:**
    - Mission and Vision: Clearly state your business's mission, vision, and long-term objectives.
    - Market Analysis: Include a detailed analysis of your industry, target market, and competitors. Explain your market position and strategy for gaining a competitive advantage.
    - Marketing and Sales Strategies: Outline your marketing plan, sales strategy, and how you plan to attract and retain customers.
    - Organizational Structure: Provide an organizational chart showing key management roles and responsibilities.
    - Financial Plan: Include financial projections (income statements, balance sheets, and cash flow statements) for at least three to five years. Explain how the loan will impact these projections.

2. **Financial Statements:**
    - Historical Financials: Provide financial statements for the past three years, including balance sheets, income statements, and cash flow statements.
    - Interim Financials: If applicable, provide interim financial statements for the current year to show recent performance.

3. **Tax Returns:**
    - Business Tax Returns: Submit your business tax returns for the past three years.

- Personal Tax Returns: Provide personal tax returns for all owners with a 20% or greater stake in the business for the past three years.

4. **Legal Documents:**
    - Business Licenses: Include copies of all business licenses and registrations required to operate legally.
    - Articles of Incorporation: Provide your articles of incorporation or organization.
    - Leases and Contracts: Submit copies of any significant leases or contracts that impact your business operations.
    - Franchise Agreements: If applicable, include franchise agreements.

5. **Personal Financial Statements:**
    - Owners' Personal Financial Statements: Provide personal financial statements for all owners with a significant stake in the business. Include details of personal assets, liabilities, and net worth.

6. **Collateral Documentation:**
    - Collateral Description: Prepare a detailed description of the assets you are willing to use as collateral. This should include appraisals, ownership documents, and any relevant valuations.

By meticulously assessing your business needs, understanding the SBA's eligibility requirements, and gathering all necessary documentation, you will be well-prepared to apply for an SBA loan. This thorough preparation not only enhances your chances of approval but also ensures that the loan will effectively support your business's growth and success.

Chapter 3: The SBA Loan Application Process

Navigating the SBA (Small Business Administration) loan application process can be a daunting task. This chapter will provide you with a comprehensive, step-by-step guide to completing your SBA loan application, ensuring you are well-prepared at every stage.

Step-by-Step Guide to Completing the SBA Loan Application

Pre-Application Preparation

Before diving into the application process, it is crucial to gather all necessary documents and assess your eligibility. This preparation stage will save you time and prevent potential delays. Here's what you need to do:

1. **Gather Necessary Documents**: Collect financial statements, tax returns, business plans, and any other documents that the SBA requires. This typically includes:
    - Personal and business tax returns (last three years)
    - Personal and business financial statements
    - Business licenses
    - Loan application history
    - Résumés for each principal
    - A detailed business plan
    - A business lease (if applicable)

2. **Assess Your Eligibility**: Different SBA loan programs have different eligibility requirements. Ensure that your business meets the basic criteria, which generally include:
    - Operating as a for-profit business
    - Doing business (or proposing to do business) in the U.S. or its territories
    - Having reasonable owner equity to invest
    - Demonstrating a need for a loan that you could not obtain on reasonable terms from other sources

Choose the Right SBA Loan Program

The SBA offers various loan programs, each designed to meet specific needs. Identifying the right program is critical:

1. **SBA 7(a) Loan Program**: Ideal for businesses seeking working capital, purchasing inventory, or refinancing debt. It is the most common and versatile SBA loan program.
2. **SBA 504 Loan Program**: Designed for businesses looking to purchase fixed assets like real estate or equipment. This program is suitable for businesses aiming for expansion or modernization.
3. **SBA Microloan Program**: Provides smaller loans up to $50,000, typically used for working capital, inventory, supplies, furniture, fixtures, machinery, or equipment.
4. **SBA Disaster Loans**: Available for businesses that have been affected by declared disasters. These loans can be used to repair or replace real estate, personal property, machinery, equipment, and other business assets.

Complete the Loan Application Form

Filling out the SBA loan application form accurately and completely is crucial. Follow these steps:

1. **Download the Correct Form**: Ensure you have the right application form for the loan program you have chosen. Forms can be found on the SBA website or obtained from your lender.
2. **Provide Accurate Information**: Fill out the form with precise details about your business, including:
    - Legal name and contact information
    - Business structure (sole proprietorship, partnership, corporation, etc.)
    - Date business was established
    - Number of employees
    - Annual revenue and net profit
    - Detailed loan request (amount and purpose)
3. **Be Thorough**: Answer every question completely. Missing information can delay the processing of your application.

Prepare Supporting Documentation

Your application will require a comprehensive set of supporting documents to verify the information you've provided. Here's a checklist of what you might need:

1. **Personal Background and Financial Statement**: Complete and sign SBA Form 912 and SBA Form 413.

2. **Business Financial Statements**: Include profit and loss statements, balance sheets, and projected financial statements.

3. **Ownership and Affiliations**: Provide a list of names and addresses of any subsidiaries and affiliates, including concerns in which the applicant holds a controlling interest and other concerns that may be affiliated by stock ownership, franchise, or otherwise.

4. **Business Certificate/License**: Provide a copy of your business certificate or license.

5. **Loan Application History**: Include records of any loans you may have applied for in the past.

6. **Income Tax Returns**: Include signed personal and business federal income tax returns for the previous three years.

7. **Résumé**: Provide personal résumés for each principal.

8. **Business Lease**: Include a copy of your business lease, if applicable.

Submit Your Application

Once your application and supporting documents are ready, submit them to an SBA-approved lender. Here's how:

1. **Find an SBA-Approved Lender**: Use the SBA Lender Match tool or contact your local SBA district office to find approved lenders.

2. **Submit Electronically or In Person**: Depending on the lender's process, you may submit your application electronically or in person.

3. **Follow Up**: Stay in contact with your lender throughout the process. They may require additional information or clarification.

Tips for Ensuring Accuracy and Completeness

To increase the likelihood of your application being approved, follow these tips:

1. **Double-Check All Information**: Ensure all data on your application is accurate. Any discrepancies can lead to delays or rejection.

2. **Include All Required Documents**: Verify that you have included all the necessary supporting documents. Use a checklist to make sure nothing is missing.

3. **Provide Clear and Concise Answers**: Be straightforward and detailed in your responses. Avoid vague or incomplete answers.

4. **Review Your Application with a Trusted Advisor or Financial Professional**: Before submitting, have a trusted advisor or financial professional review your application. They can provide valuable feedback and help you spot any errors or omissions.

By following these steps and tips, you can streamline the SBA loan application process, reduce the likelihood of errors, and enhance your chances of securing the financing your business needs.

Chapter 4: Writing a Strong Business Plan

Creating a comprehensive and detailed business plan is crucial for laying the foundation of a successful business. It serves as a blueprint for your business, helping you to organize your thoughts, identify potential challenges, and attract investors. This chapter will guide you through each key component of a business plan, explain how to highlight your business's strengths, and provide tips on developing realistic financial projections.

Key Components of a Business Plan

1. Executive Summary

The Executive Summary is the first section of your business plan, but it should be written last. This section provides a snapshot of your entire business plan and should captivate the reader's attention. It includes:

- **Business Overview**: Briefly describe what your business does. Include the name of your business, its location, and the industry it operates in.
- **Mission Statement**: Clearly state your business's mission. This should convey the purpose and values of your business.
- **Business Objectives**: Outline the short-term and long-term goals of your business. These should be specific, measurable, achievable, relevant, and time-bound (SMART).
- **Products or Services**: Summarize the main products or services you offer.
- **Target Market**: Provide a high-level overview of your target market.
- **Competitive Advantages**: Highlight what makes your business unique and how it stands out from the competition.
- **Financial Highlights**: Present key financial projections such as expected revenue, profit margins, and funding requirements.
- **Funding Requirements**: If seeking funding, briefly state how much you need and how you intend to use the funds.

2. Business Description

This section provides a detailed description of your business. It should help the reader understand your business's background, purpose, and the needs it addresses. Include the following:

- **Company Overview**: Name, location, and legal structure (e.g., sole proprietorship, partnership, corporation) of your business.

- **History**: If your business is already established, provide a brief history, including key milestones.
- **Mission Statement**: Expand on the mission statement provided in the Executive Summary.
- **Business Model**: Describe your business model and how you intend to make money.
- **Products and Services**: Provide a detailed description of your products or services, including features, benefits, and any unique selling points.
- **Customer Needs**: Explain the specific needs your business addresses and how your products or services fulfill these needs.
- **Future Plans**: Outline your future plans and growth strategy. This could include plans for product expansion, entering new markets, or increasing market share.

3. Market Analysis

Conducting a thorough market analysis is critical to understanding your industry, target market, and competition. This section should be well-researched and data-driven. Include:

- **Industry Overview**: Describe the industry your business operates in. Include information on market size, growth trends, and key drivers.
- **Target Market**: Define your target market in detail. This should include demographics (age, gender, income, education), psychographics (lifestyle, values, interests), and geographic information.
- **Market Needs**: Identify the specific needs and pain points of your target market.
- **Market Trends**: Analyze current market trends and how they may impact your business.
- **Competitive Analysis**: Identify your main competitors and analyze their strengths and weaknesses. Include information on their market share, pricing strategies, distribution channels, and marketing tactics.
- **Market Opportunities**: Highlight any gaps in the market that your business can exploit. This could include underserved customer segments, emerging trends, or areas where competitors are weak.

4. Organization and Management

This section provides an overview of your business's organizational structure and introduces your management team. It should convey that your business is well-organized and led by a capable team. Include:

- **Organizational Structure**: Present an organizational chart that shows the hierarchy and key roles within your business.
- **Management Team**: Provide detailed biographies of your management team. Highlight their qualifications, experience, and any relevant achievements.
- **Ownership Structure**: Explain the ownership structure of your business. Include information on the founders, shareholders, and any major investors.
- **Board of Directors**: If applicable, provide information on your board of directors or advisory board. Include their backgrounds and the value they bring to your business.
- **Roles and Responsibilities**: Clearly define the roles and responsibilities of each key team member. This helps to show that your business has the right people in place to execute its strategy.

5. Marketing and Sales Strategy

A well-thought-out marketing and sales strategy is essential for attracting and retaining customers. This section should outline your plans for reaching your target market and achieving your sales goals. Include:

- **Marketing Strategy**: Describe your overall marketing strategy and how it aligns with your business objectives. Include information on your brand positioning, value proposition, and key messages.
- **Target Audience**: Define your target audience in detail. Explain why they are likely to buy your products or services.
- **Marketing Channels**: Identify the marketing channels you will use to reach your target audience. This could include digital marketing (social media, email, SEO), traditional marketing (print, TV, radio), or a combination of both.
- **Marketing Tactics**: Detail the specific marketing tactics you will use to promote your business. This could include content marketing, influencer partnerships, promotions, and events.
- **Sales Strategy**: Outline your sales strategy, including your sales process, sales goals, and key performance indicators (KPIs).
- **Pricing Strategy**: Explain your pricing strategy and how it supports your overall business objectives. Include information on any discounts, promotions, or loyalty programs.
- **Distribution Channels**: Describe the distribution channels you will use to deliver your products or services to customers. This could include online sales, retail stores, wholesalers, or direct sales.

6. Product Line or Services

This section provides a detailed description of your products or services. It should help the reader understand what you offer and why it is valuable to your target market. Include:

- **Product/Service Description**: Provide a detailed description of each product or service you offer. Include information on the features, benefits, and unique selling points.
- **Product/Service Development**: Explain the development process for your products or services. Include information on any research and development (R&D) activities, prototypes, and testing.
- **Product Lifecycle**: Describe the lifecycle stage of each product or service. This could include information on new product launches, growth, maturity, and potential decline.
- **Intellectual Property**: Provide information on any intellectual property (IP) your business owns. This could include patents, trademarks, copyrights, or trade secrets.
- **Future Products/Services**: Outline any plans for future products or services. Explain how these will complement your existing offerings and support your growth strategy.

7. Funding Request

If you are seeking funding, this section should clearly outline your funding requirements and how you intend to use the funds. Include:

- **Funding Amount**: Specify the amount of funding you need and the type of funding you are seeking (e.g., equity, debt, grants).
- **Use of Funds**: Provide a detailed breakdown of how you will use the funds. This could include marketing, product development, hiring, equipment, or working capital.
- **Funding Timeline**: Outline the timeline for when you need the funds and any milestones or deliverables associated with the funding.
- **Future Funding Requirements**: If applicable, provide information on any future funding requirements and how you plan to meet them.
- **Exit Strategy**: Explain your exit strategy if you are seeking equity funding. This could include plans for an initial public offering (IPO), acquisition, or buyout.

8. Financial Projections

Financial projections are critical for demonstrating the financial viability of your business. This section should provide detailed forecasts and show that your business is financially sound. Include:

- **Income Statements**: Provide projected income statements for the next three to five years. Include information on revenue, cost of goods sold (COGS), gross profit, operating expenses, and net profit.
- **Cash Flow Statements**: Provide projected cash flow statements for the next three to five years. Include information on cash inflows and outflows, operating activities, investing activities, and financing activities.
- **Balance Sheets**: Provide projected balance sheets for the next three to five years. Include information on assets, liabilities, and equity.
- **Break-Even Analysis**: Conduct a break-even analysis to determine when your business will become profitable. Include information on fixed costs, variable costs, and break-even sales volume.
- **Sales Forecasts**: Provide detailed sales forecasts for each product or service. Include information on pricing, sales volume, and revenue.
- **Expense Budgets**: Provide detailed expense budgets for your business. Include information on operating expenses, marketing expenses, and any other significant costs.
- **Financial Assumptions**: Clearly state the assumptions underlying your financial projections. This could include market growth rates, pricing assumptions, and cost estimates.

9. Appendix

The appendix is the final section of your business plan. It should include any additional supporting documents that strengthen your plan. Include:

- **Resumes**: Provide resumes of your management team and key employees.
- **Product Photos/Prototypes**: Include photos or prototypes of your products.
- **Market Research Data**: Provide detailed market research data and analysis.
- **Legal Documents**: Include any legal documents, such as contracts, permits, or intellectual property filings.
- **References/Endorsements**: Include letters of reference or endorsement from customers, partners, or industry experts.

How to Highlight Your Business's Strengths

Emphasize Your Unique Selling Points

Your unique selling points (USPs) are what differentiate your business from the competition. Clearly articulate these in your business plan to show why customers should choose your products or services. This could include:

- **Superior Product Quality**: Highlight any unique features or superior quality of your products.
- **Innovative Features**: Showcase any innovative features or technology that set your products apart.
- **Exceptional Customer Service**: Emphasize your commitment to customer service and how it benefits your customers.
- **Unique Business Model**: Explain any unique aspects of your business model that provide a competitive advantage.

Highlight Your Business's Competitive Advantages

Your competitive advantages are the strengths that enable your business to compete effectively in the market. Highlight these in your business plan to show why your business is positioned to succeed. This could include:

- **Proprietary Technology/Processes**: Highlight any proprietary technology or processes that give your business an edge.
- **Strategic Partnerships**: Showcase any strategic partnerships or alliances that strengthen your business.
- **Strong Brand Recognition**: Emphasize any strong brand recognition or market presence your business has.
- **Cost Advantages**: Highlight any cost advantages or efficiencies that enable your business to compete on price.

Showcase Your Management Team's Experience and Expertise

A strong management team is critical to the success of your business. Highlight the experience and expertise of your management team to build confidence with investors and stakeholders. This could include:

- **Relevant Industry Experience**: Emphasize any relevant industry experience your management team has.
- **Past Successes**: Highlight any past successes or achievements of your management team.
- **Unique Skills/Expertise**: Showcase any unique skills or expertise that add value to your business.

Financial Projections and Supporting Data

Provide Realistic and Well-Researched Financial Projections

Your financial projections should be realistic and based on thorough research. This builds credibility and confidence in your business plan. Include:

- **Revenue Projections**: Provide detailed revenue projections based on realistic assumptions.
- **Expense Projections**: Provide detailed expense projections, including both fixed and variable costs.
- **Profit Margins**: Calculate your expected profit margins and explain how you plan to achieve them.
- **Growth Rates**: Provide realistic growth rates based on market research and industry trends.
- **Sensitivity Analysis**: Conduct a sensitivity analysis to show how changes in key assumptions could impact your financial projections.

Include Supporting Data to Back Up Your Projections

Supporting data is critical for validating your financial projections. Include:

- **Market Research Data**: Provide detailed market research data to support your revenue projections.
- **Historical Financial Data**: If your business is already established, include historical financial data to support your projections.
- **Comparable Financial Performance**: Provide information on the financial performance of similar businesses to validate your projections.

Use Conservative Estimates to Demonstrate Financial Prudence

Using conservative estimates in your financial projections shows that you are aware of potential risks and have a realistic outlook. This approach helps to build trust with investors and stakeholders. Include:

- **Conservative Revenue Projections**: Use conservative estimates for your revenue projections to account for potential market fluctuations.
- **Contingency Plans**: Include contingency plans to address potential risks and challenges.
- **Prudent Cost Estimates**: Use conservative estimates for your cost projections to ensure that you have a buffer for unexpected expenses.

By meticulously detailing each component of your business plan and highlighting your business's strengths, you create a comprehensive and compelling document that can attract investors, guide your strategy, and drive your business's success.

Chapter 5: Financial Statements and Projections

Preparing Your Financial Statements

Financial statements are essential tools for understanding the financial health and performance of your business. They provide critical insights that help you make informed decisions, attract investors, and secure financing. In this chapter, we will detail the three primary financial statements you need to prepare and their importance.

Income Statement

The income statement, also known as the profit and loss statement, shows your business's profitability over a specific period, typically a quarter or a year. It provides a summary of revenues, costs, and expenses incurred during a particular period. Here's a breakdown of what an income statement includes:

1. **Revenue:** The total income generated from the sale of goods or services.
2. **Cost of Goods Sold (COGS):** The direct costs attributable to the production of the goods sold by the company.
3. **Gross Profit:** Calculated as Revenue minus COGS.
4. **Operating Expenses:** Expenses related to the core operations of the business, such as salaries, rent, and utilities.
5. **Operating Income:** Gross Profit minus Operating Expenses.
6. **Net Income:** The final profit after all expenses, taxes, and interest have been deducted from the total revenue.

By analyzing the income statement, you can determine how well your business is performing in terms of profitability and identify areas where costs can be managed or reduced.

Balance Sheet

The balance sheet provides a snapshot of your business's financial position at a specific point in time. It details your assets, liabilities, and equity, offering a clear picture of what your business owns and owes. The balance sheet is divided into three main sections:

1. **Assets:** Resources owned by the business that have economic value. They are categorized into:
    - Current Assets: Cash and other assets expected to be converted to cash within a year (e.g., accounts receivable, inventory).
    - Fixed Assets: Long-term resources such as equipment, buildings, and land.
2. **Liabilities:** Obligations or debts the business owes to others. They are divided into:

- Current Liabilities: Debts payable within a year (e.g., accounts payable, short-term loans).
- Long-term Liabilities: Debts payable over a longer period (e.g., mortgages, long-term loans).

3. **Equity:** The residual interest in the assets of the business after deducting liabilities. It represents the owner's claim on the business.

A well-prepared balance sheet helps you understand the liquidity, financial flexibility, and overall financial health of your business.

Cash Flow Statement

The cash flow statement tracks the flow of cash in and out of your business over a specific period. It highlights how well your business manages its cash position, providing insights into your ability to meet short-term obligations and sustain operations. The cash flow statement is divided into three main sections:

1. **Operating Activities:** Cash flows from the core business operations, including cash receipts from sales and cash payments for goods and services.
2. **Investing Activities:** Cash flows related to the acquisition or sale of long-term assets, such as equipment and real estate.
3. **Financing Activities:** Cash flows from transactions with the business's owners and creditors, such as issuing shares or repaying loans.

By maintaining a detailed cash flow statement, you can ensure your business has sufficient cash to operate and identify potential cash flow issues before they become critical.

Creating Realistic Financial Projections

Financial projections are forward-looking statements that estimate your business's future financial performance. They are crucial for planning, securing financing, and managing growth. Here's how to create realistic financial projections:

1. **Base Projections on Historical Data and Realistic Assumptions:**
   - Use past financial performance as a foundation for your projections.
   - Make realistic assumptions about future sales, expenses, and market conditions.
   - Consider industry trends and economic factors that could impact your business.
2. **Include Projected Financial Statements:**
   - **Projected Income Statements:** Estimate future revenues, expenses, and profitability.

- o **Projected Balance Sheets:** Forecast your future assets, liabilities, and equity.
- o **Projected Cash Flow Statements:** Predict future cash inflows and outflows to ensure liquidity.

3. **Explain and Justify Your Projections:**
   - o Be prepared to provide detailed explanations and justifications for your assumptions and projections.
   - o Present supporting data, market research, and analysis to lenders and investors.
   - o Demonstrate how your projections align with your business plan and strategic goals.

Importance of a Cash Flow Statement

The cash flow statement is a critical financial document for several reasons:

1. **Demonstrates Ability to Generate Cash and Meet Financial Obligations:**
   - o Shows how efficiently your business generates cash from operations.
   - o Highlights your ability to pay suppliers, employees, and creditors on time.

2. **Helps Lenders Assess Financial Health and Sustainability:**
   - o Provides lenders with a clear picture of your business's liquidity and financial stability.
   - o Assists in evaluating the risk associated with lending to your business.

3. **Provides Insights into Operational Efficiency:**
   - o Helps identify areas where cash flow can be improved.
   - o Enables you to manage working capital more effectively and make informed decisions about investments and financing.

By thoroughly preparing your financial statements and creating realistic financial projections, you can better understand your business's financial health, plan for the future, and attract the necessary funding to achieve your goals.

4o

much more detailed

ChatGPT

Chapter 5: Financial Statements and Projections

Preparing Your Financial Statements

Financial statements are the cornerstone of any business's financial management and planning. They provide detailed insights into the business's financial performance and position, enabling informed decision-making, effective planning, and securing investments. This chapter will delve into the preparation of the three primary financial statements: the income statement, balance sheet, and cash flow statement.

Income Statement

The income statement, also known as the profit and loss statement, illustrates your business's profitability over a specific period, usually quarterly or annually. It details revenues, expenses, and profits or losses, providing a comprehensive view of your business's financial performance.

Components of an Income Statement:

1. **Revenue:**
    - Total income generated from the sale of goods or services.
    - Includes all sales revenue, net of returns, allowances, and discounts.
2. **Cost of Goods Sold (COGS):**
    - Direct costs attributable to the production of goods sold.
    - Includes raw materials, direct labor, and manufacturing overhead.
3. **Gross Profit:**
    - Calculated as Revenue minus COGS.
    - Indicates the efficiency of production and pricing strategies.
4. **Operating Expenses:**
    - Costs incurred during normal business operations.
    - Includes salaries, rent, utilities, marketing, and administrative expenses.
5. **Operating Income:**
    - Gross Profit minus Operating Expenses.
    - Reflects the profitability of core business operations.
6. **Non-Operating Items:**
    - Includes interest expense, taxes, and any extraordinary items.
    - Reflects income or expenses not directly related to core business operations.

7. **Net Income:**
    - The final profit after all expenses, taxes, and interest have been deducted from total revenue.
    - Indicates overall profitability and is a key indicator for stakeholders.

Steps to Prepare an Income Statement:

1. **Gather Financial Data:**
    - Collect all revenue and expense data for the period.
    - Ensure all transactions are accurately recorded in the accounting system.
2. **Calculate Revenue:**
    - Sum up all income generated from sales of goods and services.
3. **Determine COGS:**
    - Calculate the total cost of production, including direct labor and materials.
4. **Compute Gross Profit:**
    - Subtract COGS from total revenue.
5. **List Operating Expenses:**
    - Itemize all operational costs and sum them up.
6. **Calculate Operating Income:**
    - Subtract total operating expenses from gross profit.
7. **Incorporate Non-Operating Items:**
    - Add any additional income and subtract non-operating expenses.
8. **Determine Net Income:**
    - Calculate the final net income by subtracting non-operating items from operating income.

Balance Sheet

The balance sheet provides a snapshot of your business's financial position at a specific point in time. It details what your business owns (assets), what it owes (liabilities), and the owner's equity, offering a comprehensive overview of financial stability and structure.

Components of a Balance Sheet:

1. **Assets:**
   - **Current Assets:** Cash and other assets expected to be converted to cash within a year (e.g., accounts receivable, inventory).
   - **Fixed Assets:** Long-term resources such as property, plant, equipment, and intangible assets.
2. **Liabilities:**
   - **Current Liabilities:** Debts payable within a year (e.g., accounts payable, short-term loans).
   - **Long-term Liabilities:** Debts payable over a longer period (e.g., mortgages, long-term loans).
3. **Equity:**
   - The residual interest in the assets of the business after deducting liabilities.
   - Includes retained earnings and capital contributions by owners.

Steps to Prepare a Balance Sheet:

1. **List Assets:**
   - Itemize all current and fixed assets, including their values.
2. **List Liabilities:**
   - Itemize all current and long-term liabilities, including their values.
3. **Calculate Equity:**
   - Subtract total liabilities from total assets to determine equity.
4. **Format the Balance Sheet:**
   - Organize the balance sheet into the three sections: assets, liabilities, and equity.
   - Ensure that total assets equal the sum of total liabilities and equity.

Cash Flow Statement

The cash flow statement tracks the flow of cash in and out of your business over a specific period. It highlights your ability to generate cash, manage liquidity, and meet financial obligations, providing a detailed view of operational efficiency and financial health.

Components of a Cash Flow Statement:

1. **Operating Activities:**

- Cash flows from core business operations.
- Includes cash receipts from sales and cash payments for goods and services.

2. **Investing Activities:**
   - Cash flows related to the acquisition or sale of long-term assets.
   - Includes purchases of equipment and real estate transactions.

3. **Financing Activities:**
   - Cash flows from transactions with the business's owners and creditors.
   - Includes issuing shares, repaying loans, and dividend payments.

Steps to Prepare a Cash Flow Statement:

1. **Collect Cash Flow Data:**
   - Gather all cash transactions for the period, categorized into operating, investing, and financing activities.

2. **Calculate Cash Flow from Operating Activities:**
   - Adjust net income for changes in working capital and non-cash expenses (e.g., depreciation).

3. **Calculate Cash Flow from Investing Activities:**
   - Record cash used for asset purchases and cash received from asset sales.

4. **Calculate Cash Flow from Financing Activities:**
   - Record cash inflows from issuing shares or taking loans and outflows from repaying debt and paying dividends.

5. **Compile the Cash Flow Statement:**
   - Combine the cash flows from operating, investing, and financing activities to determine the net increase or decrease in cash.

Creating Realistic Financial Projections

Financial projections are forward-looking statements that estimate your business's future financial performance. They are essential for planning, securing financing, and managing growth. Here's how to create realistic financial projections:

Steps to Create Financial Projections:

1. **Base Projections on Historical Data and Realistic Assumptions:**

- **Analyze Historical Data:** Use past financial performance as a foundation for your projections. Identify trends and patterns in revenue, expenses, and profitability.
- **Make Realistic Assumptions:** Consider industry trends, market conditions, and economic factors. Ensure assumptions are based on solid data and reasonable expectations.
- **Scenario Analysis:** Develop multiple scenarios (e.g., best-case, worst-case, and most likely) to account for uncertainties and potential risks.

2. **Include Projected Financial Statements:**
   - **Projected Income Statements:** Estimate future revenues, COGS, operating expenses, and net income.
   - **Projected Balance Sheets:** Forecast future assets, liabilities, and equity. Consider capital expenditures, debt repayments, and equity financing.
   - **Projected Cash Flow Statements:** Predict future cash inflows and outflows. Include detailed projections for operating, investing, and financing activities.

3. **Explain and Justify Your Projections:**
   - **Provide Supporting Data:** Present market research, industry reports, and internal data to justify assumptions. Highlight key drivers of revenue and cost projections.
   - **Align with Business Plan:** Ensure projections align with your business plan and strategic goals. Demonstrate how projected financial performance supports your growth and operational strategies.
   - **Prepare for Scrutiny:** Be prepared to explain and justify your projections to lenders, investors, and stakeholders. Anticipate questions and provide detailed explanations for key assumptions and projections.

Importance of a Cash Flow Statement

The cash flow statement is a critical financial document for several reasons:

1. **Demonstrates Ability to Generate Cash and Meet Financial Obligations:**
   - **Operational Efficiency:** Shows how efficiently your business generates cash from operations, highlighting the effectiveness of your business model.
   - **Liquidity Management:** Helps ensure you have sufficient cash to cover short-term obligations, such as paying suppliers, employees, and creditors.

2. **Helps Lenders Assess Financial Health and Sustainability:**

- **Risk Assessment:** Provides lenders with a clear picture of your business's liquidity and financial stability. Helps them assess the risk associated with lending to your business.
- **Creditworthiness:** Demonstrates your ability to generate cash and meet debt obligations, enhancing your creditworthiness and ability to secure financing.

3. **Provides Insights into Operational Efficiency:**
   - **Cash Flow Trends:** Helps identify trends in cash flow, such as seasonal fluctuations or changes in working capital requirements. Enables proactive management of cash flow issues.
   - **Investment Decisions:** Provides insights into the availability of cash for reinvestment in the business. Helps evaluate the financial feasibility of capital expenditures and growth initiatives.

By thoroughly preparing your financial statements and creating realistic financial projections, you can better understand your business's financial health, plan for the future, and attract the necessary funding to achieve your goals. These tools are indispensable for managing your business's growth, securing financing, and ensuring long-term sustainability.

Chapter 6: Collateral and Personal Guarantees

Securing a business loan can be a multifaceted process, and understanding the requirements for collateral and personal guarantees is crucial for a successful application. This chapter will provide a comprehensive explanation of what collateral and personal guarantees entail, the types of acceptable collateral, and the significance of personal guarantees in the loan approval process.

Understanding Collateral Requirements

Collateral is an asset that you pledge as security for a loan. It serves as a form of protection for the lender, ensuring that they can recover the loan amount if the borrower defaults. Collateral not only increases the likelihood of loan approval but also can result in more favorable loan terms, such as lower interest rates and longer repayment periods. The value and type of collateral you provide can significantly impact the terms of your loan.

The primary purpose of collateral is to reduce the risk for the lender. In case the borrower fails to repay the loan, the lender can seize the collateral and sell it to recover the outstanding loan amount. This security helps the lender mitigate potential losses, making them more inclined to approve the loan.

Types of Acceptable Collateral

Different lenders may have varying requirements for what constitutes acceptable collateral. Here are some common types of collateral that businesses can use:

1. **Real Estate:**
   - **Commercial Property:** This includes office buildings, warehouses, retail spaces, and any other real estate used for business purposes. Commercial property is often considered highly valuable collateral due to its potential for appreciation and stable market demand.
   - **Personal Property:** Residential properties owned by the business owner can also be used as collateral, although this is less common. Using personal property as collateral involves significant risk, as defaulting on the loan could result in losing one's home.

2. **Equipment:**
   - This category includes machinery, vehicles, and other equipment essential to your business operations. The equipment must have a clear market value and be in good working condition. Lenders typically prefer equipment that is easily sellable and has a relatively stable market value.

3. **Inventory:**

- Inventory refers to the products or materials that your business sells. This can include raw materials, finished goods, or merchandise. The inventory must be easily sellable and not perishable or obsolete. Lenders will assess the turnover rate of the inventory and its current market value to determine its suitability as collateral.

4. **Accounts Receivable:**
    - Accounts receivable represent the money owed to your business by customers for goods or services provided. Lenders may consider this type of collateral if the receivables are from creditworthy customers and have a predictable payment history. The age of the receivables and the creditworthiness of the customers will be critical factors in the lender's evaluation.

Personal Guarantees: What They Are and Why They Matter

A personal guarantee is a legal commitment by the business owner to repay a loan if the business itself is unable to do so. It is a significant factor in the loan approval process for several reasons:

1. **Reduces Lender's Risk:**
    - By providing a personal guarantee, the business owner assures the lender that they are committed to repaying the loan, even if the business faces financial difficulties. This reduces the lender's risk and makes them more willing to approve the loan. Personal guarantees demonstrate the borrower's confidence in their business's future performance and their personal commitment to its success.

2. **Increases Chances of Loan Approval:**
    - Lenders are more likely to approve loans when the borrower provides a personal guarantee because it demonstrates the owner's confidence in their business's ability to repay the loan. It also indicates that the owner has a personal stake in the business's success. Lenders often view personal guarantees as a sign of the owner's credibility and trustworthiness.

3. **Be Prepared to Provide a Personal Guarantee:**
    - Many lenders, especially for small businesses or startups, require personal guarantees as a standard part of the loan process. Business owners should be prepared to offer this guarantee and understand the implications fully. If the business defaults on the loan, the lender can pursue the owner's personal assets, such as savings, investments, or other property, to recover the outstanding debt. This means that in the event of default, the business owner's personal finances and assets are at risk, making it essential to carefully consider the potential consequences before agreeing to a personal guarantee.

Steps to Prepare for Collateral and Personal Guarantees

1. **Evaluate Your Assets:**
   - Assess the value and liquidity of your assets. Determine which assets you can feasibly pledge as collateral without significantly disrupting your business operations. Create a detailed inventory of potential collateral and gather documentation to prove ownership and value.

2. **Understand Your Loan Requirements:**
   - Research and understand the specific collateral and personal guarantee requirements of different lenders. Each lender may have unique criteria, and being well-informed can help you tailor your application to meet their expectations.

3. **Consult Financial Advisors:**
   - Engage with financial advisors or loan specialists to get a clear understanding of the risks and benefits associated with pledging collateral and providing personal guarantees. They can offer valuable insights and help you make informed decisions.

4. **Prepare Necessary Documentation:**
   - Ensure you have all the necessary documentation to prove the value and ownership of your collateral. This may include property deeds, equipment appraisals, inventory lists, and accounts receivable aging reports. Proper documentation can streamline the loan approval process.

5. **Negotiate Terms:**
   - Don't hesitate to negotiate the terms of the loan, including the collateral requirements and the scope of the personal guarantee. A well-prepared and informed borrower can often secure more favorable terms by demonstrating their knowledge and commitment.

Understanding the requirements and implications of collateral and personal guarantees is essential for any business owner seeking a loan. Properly preparing and providing the necessary collateral and being ready to offer a personal guarantee can significantly improve your chances of securing the funding you need to grow and sustain your business. Always weigh the potential risks and benefits carefully, and seek professional advice to navigate this complex aspect of business financing.

Chapter 7: Working with an SBA-Approved Lender

Securing financing for your business through the Small Business Administration (SBA) can provide numerous benefits, including access to favorable loan terms and a higher chance of approval. However, navigating the SBA loan process requires working with an SBA-approved lender. This chapter will guide you through the essential steps of finding the right lender, building a strong relationship with them, and understanding what they look for in a loan application.

Finding the Right Lender

1. **Look for Lenders with Experience in SBA Lending**

When searching for a lender, it is crucial to prioritize those with a proven track record in SBA lending. These lenders are well-versed in the intricacies of the SBA loan process and can guide you more effectively through the application and approval stages. To identify such lenders:

- **Research Online**: Use the SBA's Lender Match tool and other online resources to find a list of SBA-approved lenders. Look for lenders with a high volume of SBA loan approvals and positive reviews from other borrowers.
- **Ask for Recommendations**: Speak with other business owners in your network who have successfully secured SBA loans. They can provide valuable insights and recommend lenders with whom they had positive experiences.
- **Evaluate Experience**: Check the lender's experience with the specific SBA loan programs that fit your needs, such as the 7(a) loan, 504 loan, or microloans.

2. **Consider Factors such as Interest Rates, Fees, and Customer Service**

Beyond their experience, it is essential to evaluate potential lenders based on key financial and service factors:

- **Interest Rates**: Compare the interest rates offered by different lenders. While SBA loans typically have lower rates than conventional loans, there can still be variations. Lower rates can significantly reduce the overall cost of your loan over time.
- **Fees**: Be aware of any upfront fees, ongoing service fees, or penalties for early repayment. These fees can add to the cost of your loan. Some common fees include origination fees, application fees, and closing costs. Ask each lender for a detailed breakdown of all potential fees.
- **Customer Service**: Assess the quality of customer service. Responsive and supportive lenders can make a significant difference, especially if issues arise

during the loan term. Look for lenders who are willing to answer your questions promptly, provide clear explanations, and offer personalized guidance.

Building a Relationship with Your Lender

1. **Communicate Openly and Honestly with Your Lender**

Transparency is crucial in your dealings with your lender. Share all relevant information about your business, including both strengths and weaknesses. Open communication helps build trust and allows the lender to provide better guidance and support. To foster transparency:

- **Regular Updates**: Keep your lender informed about significant business developments, such as new contracts, major purchases, or changes in management.
- **Address Issues Promptly**: If you encounter challenges, such as cash flow problems or unexpected expenses, inform your lender immediately. They may be able to offer solutions or adjustments to your loan terms.

2. **Provide Timely and Accurate Information**

Ensure that all information you provide is accurate and up-to-date. Inaccuracies or delays can hinder the loan process and damage your credibility. Timely submission of required documents and information demonstrates your reliability and commitment. Key documents may include:

- **Financial Statements**: Regularly updated balance sheets, income statements, and cash flow statements.
- **Tax Returns**: Both personal and business tax returns for the past few years.
- **Business Plan**: An updated business plan that reflects your current operations and future goals.

3. **Foster a Positive and Collaborative Relationship**

View your relationship with your lender as a partnership. Approach interactions with a cooperative attitude and be receptive to their advice and feedback. A positive, collaborative relationship can facilitate smoother negotiations and better support throughout the loan term. To build this relationship:

- **Engage Regularly**: Schedule regular meetings or check-ins with your lender to discuss your business performance and any potential issues.
- **Show Appreciation**: Acknowledge your lender's support and express gratitude for their assistance. Building rapport can lead to more favorable terms and conditions in the future.

What Lenders Look For in an Application

1. **Strong Credit History and Financial Stability**

Lenders assess your credit history to gauge your reliability in repaying debts. A strong credit score and a history of timely payments are indicators of financial responsibility. Additionally, lenders will evaluate your business's financial stability, including cash flow, revenue trends, and profitability. To strengthen your application:

- o **Review Your Credit Report**: Obtain your credit report and review it for any errors. Dispute any inaccuracies that could negatively impact your score.
- o **Maintain Healthy Finances**: Ensure your business maintains positive cash flow and stable revenue. Reduce outstanding debts and avoid taking on new liabilities before applying for the loan.

2. **Clear and Convincing Business Plan**

A well-documented business plan is critical. It should clearly outline your business model, market analysis, marketing strategy, operational plan, and financial projections. Your business plan should convince the lender of your business's viability and growth potential. Key elements to include:

- o **Executive Summary**: A brief overview of your business, including its mission, vision, and objectives.
- o **Market Analysis**: Detailed research on your industry, target market, and competitive landscape.
- o **Marketing Strategy**: Plans for attracting and retaining customers, including pricing, promotion, and distribution strategies.
- o **Operational Plan**: Details on your business operations, including production processes, supply chain management, and staffing requirements.
- o **Financial Projections**: Realistic financial forecasts, including projected income statements, balance sheets, and cash flow statements for the next three to five years.

3. **Adequate Collateral and Personal Guarantees**

Lenders often require collateral to secure the loan. This can include business assets, real estate, or personal assets. Be prepared to offer sufficient collateral to cover the loan amount. Additionally, personal guarantees from business owners may be required, which makes you personally liable for the loan. To prepare:

- o **Inventory Your Assets**: List all business and personal assets that could serve as collateral. Provide accurate valuations for these assets.

- **Understand Personal Guarantees**: Be aware of the implications of personal guarantees and ensure you are comfortable with the level of personal risk involved.

4. **Demonstrated Ability to Repay the Loan**

Finally, lenders need assurance that you can repay the loan. Provide detailed financial statements, cash flow projections, and any other relevant documentation that demonstrates your ability to generate sufficient income to meet your loan obligations. Highlight any existing contracts, customer commitments, or other sources of revenue that support your repayment capacity. To demonstrate this ability:

- **Show Historical Performance**: Provide historical financial data that shows consistent revenue growth and profitability.
- **Highlight Future Opportunities**: Emphasize any new contracts, partnerships, or market expansions that will drive future revenue.

By following these guidelines, you can enhance your chances of securing an SBA loan and establish a productive relationship with your lender. Remember, the right lender can be a valuable ally in your business's growth and success.

Chapter 8: The SBA Loan Underwriting Process

Securing an SBA (Small Business Administration) loan involves a rigorous underwriting process designed to assess the viability of your business and your ability to repay the loan. This chapter provides an in-depth look at what to expect during the underwriting process, common reasons for loan denial, and strategies for addressing underwriting concerns.

What to Expect During Underwriting

The underwriting process for an SBA loan is a comprehensive evaluation that includes multiple steps and thorough scrutiny of your application. Here's what you can expect:

1. Application Review

Initial Submission

- **Document Collection**: Ensure you have submitted all required documents. This typically includes your business plan, personal and business tax returns, financial statements (balance sheet, income statement, cash flow statement), a debt schedule, a list of business assets, and personal financial statements of all business owners.
- **Document Accuracy**: Double-check for accuracy and completeness. Any errors or omissions can delay the process or lead to denial.

Detailed Examination

- **Business Plan Review**: Lenders will scrutinize your business plan to understand your business model, market strategy, competitive landscape, and growth projections. A well-articulated business plan with realistic financial projections is crucial.
- **Financial Statements**: Your financial statements should reflect a healthy and stable business. Lenders will look for consistency and positive trends in revenue, profitability, and cash flow.

2. Credit Check

Personal and Business Credit

- **Personal Credit Check**: Lenders will review your personal credit score and history. A strong personal credit score indicates responsible financial behavior.
- **Business Credit Check**: If your business has an established credit history, lenders will evaluate it to assess how your business has managed past debts and obligations.

Creditworthiness Assessment

- **Credit Score**: While each lender may have different requirements, a higher credit score generally improves your chances of approval.

- **Credit History**: Lenders will examine your credit history for red flags such as late payments, defaults, or bankruptcies.

3. Financial Analysis

In-Depth Financial Review

- **Income Statements**: Lenders will analyze your income statements to assess your revenue streams, profit margins, and overall profitability. They will look for consistent revenue growth and manageable expenses.
- **Balance Sheets**: Your balance sheets should show a strong asset base and manageable liabilities. Lenders will examine your liquidity, solvency, and overall financial health.
- **Cash Flow Statements**: Positive cash flow is critical. Lenders will review your cash flow statements to ensure your business generates enough cash to cover operational expenses and debt repayments.

Ratio Analysis

- **Debt-to-Income Ratio**: This ratio indicates your ability to manage additional debt. A lower ratio is preferable.
- **Profitability Ratios**: Ratios like net profit margin and return on assets will be assessed to gauge your business's profitability.
- **Liquidity Ratios**: Ratios such as the current ratio and quick ratio will be reviewed to determine your business's ability to meet short-term obligations.

4. Site Visit

Purpose and Scope

- **Verification**: A site visit allows the lender to verify the information provided in your application, including the state and value of any collateral.
- **Business Operations**: Lenders will observe your business operations to ensure they align with your business plan. They may look at your facilities, equipment, inventory, and overall business environment.

Impact on Decision

- **Operational Health**: A well-managed and organized operation can positively influence the lender's decision.
- **Collateral Assessment**: The condition and value of your collateral will be assessed to determine its adequacy in securing the loan.

Common Reasons for Loan Denial

Understanding the common reasons for loan denial can help you better prepare your application and address potential issues proactively. Here are some typical reasons SBA loan applications get rejected:

1. Inadequate Credit History or Poor Credit Score

Personal Credit Issues

- **Low Credit Score**: A low personal credit score suggests a higher risk to lenders.
- **Credit Report Red Flags**: Issues such as late payments, high credit utilization, defaults, or bankruptcies can negatively impact your application.

Business Credit Issues

- **Limited Business Credit History**: A lack of established business credit history can make it difficult for lenders to assess your business's creditworthiness.
- **Negative Business Credit Events**: Past issues such as late payments, defaults, or liens can be detrimental.

2. Insufficient Collateral or Personal Guarantees

Collateral Value

- **Inadequate Collateral**: If the collateral you offer does not cover the loan amount, lenders may deny your application.
- **Depreciating Assets**: Collateral that depreciates quickly may not be sufficient to secure the loan.

Personal Guarantees

- **Lack of Guarantees**: Lenders often require personal guarantees from business owners. If you are unwilling or unable to provide these, your application may be rejected.

3. Incomplete or Inaccurate Application

Missing Information

- **Incomplete Forms**: Missing or incomplete application forms can lead to delays or denial.
- **Required Documents**: Ensure all required documents are submitted and complete.

Errors and Discrepancies

- **Inaccurate Information**: Errors or discrepancies in your application can raise red flags and lead to rejection.

- **Inconsistent Financial Data**: Ensure that all financial data is accurate and consistent across all documents.

4. Lack of Business Experience or Poor Business Plan

Business Experience

- **Insufficient Experience**: Lenders prefer applicants with a proven track record in business management and industry-specific experience.
- **Management Team**: A weak or inexperienced management team can also be a concern.

Business Plan Quality

- **Unrealistic Projections**: Overly optimistic or unrealistic financial projections can undermine the credibility of your business plan.
- **Lack of Detail**: A business plan that lacks detail or fails to address key aspects such as market analysis, competitive strategy, and operational plans can be a red flag.

How to Address Underwriting Concerns

If the lender raises concerns during the underwriting process, it's important to address them promptly and thoroughly. Here are some strategies to help you navigate these challenges:

1. Provide Additional Documentation or Clarification if Requested

Timely Response

- **Prompt Submission**: Respond promptly to any requests for additional documentation or clarification. Delays can prolong the underwriting process or lead to denial.
- **Comprehensive Information**: Ensure the additional information you provide is thorough and addresses the lender's concerns fully.

2. Be Prepared to Explain Any Discrepancies or Weaknesses in Your Application

Transparency

- **Honest Explanations**: Be honest and transparent when explaining any discrepancies or weaknesses in your application. Providing context and showing how you have addressed or plan to address these issues can help alleviate lender concerns.
- **Mitigation Plans**: Present any plans or actions you have taken to mitigate risks or improve weaknesses, such as improving cash flow, increasing revenue, or strengthening management.

3. Consider Reapplying with a Stronger Application or Different Loan Program

Strengthening Your Application

- **Improve Credit Score**: Take steps to improve your personal and business credit scores before reapplying. This might include paying down debt, correcting errors on your credit report, and maintaining timely payments.
- **Increase Collateral**: Secure additional collateral to offer more security to the lender.
- **Refine Business Plan**: Update and refine your business plan to make it more detailed and realistic.

Alternative Loan Programs

- **Explore Other Options**: Consider other SBA loan programs or alternative financing options that might be a better fit for your needs and qualifications.
- **Seek Professional Advice**: Consult with a financial advisor or loan specialist to help identify the best loan program for your situation and guide you through the application process.

By understanding the SBA loan underwriting process in detail and proactively addressing potential concerns, you can enhance your chances of securing the financing needed to grow and sustain your business.

Chapter 9: Closing the Loan

Closing a loan is a crucial and multifaceted stage in the lending process. It involves finalizing all terms and conditions agreed upon between the borrower and the lender, ensuring that all necessary documentation is accurate and complete, and addressing any last-minute issues that might arise. This chapter provides a comprehensive guide to understanding the closing process, detailing the required documentation, and offering tips for a smooth closing.

Understanding the Closing Process

1. **Commitment Letter from the Lender**

The first step in the closing process is receiving a commitment letter from your lender. This document is a formal offer that outlines the terms and conditions of the loan, including:

- **Loan Amount:** The total sum of money being borrowed.
- **Interest Rate:** The percentage charged on the loan amount, expressed annually.
- **Repayment Schedule:** Detailed information about the payment frequency (monthly, quarterly, etc.), the duration of the loan, and the due dates for each payment.
- **Special Conditions or Covenants:** Any additional requirements or restrictions imposed by the lender, such as maintaining a certain level of insurance, providing periodic financial statements, or restrictions on additional borrowing.

It is vital to review this letter meticulously to ensure that all terms match what was discussed during the loan application and negotiation stages. Any discrepancies should be immediately addressed with your loan officer.

2. **Review and Sign the Loan Agreement**

After confirming the commitment letter, the next step is to review and sign the loan agreement. This legal document formalizes your acceptance of the loan's terms and conditions and includes:

- **Loan Terms:** Detailed explanation of the loan amount, interest rate, and repayment schedule.
- **Borrower's Obligations:** Responsibilities you must fulfill, such as timely payments, maintaining collateral, and complying with any covenants.
- **Lender's Rights:** The rights of the lender in case of default, including repossession of collateral or legal actions.
- **Amendment and Waiver Clauses:** Conditions under which the terms of the loan can be amended or waived.

Thoroughly read this document, and consider seeking legal advice to fully understand the implications. Signing this agreement signifies your legal commitment to repay the loan under the specified terms.

3. **Final Credit Check and Appraisal**

Before the loan is officially closed, the lender may perform a final credit check to ensure that there have been no significant changes in your financial status since the initial approval. They may also require a final appraisal of the collateral to confirm its current value. This step ensures that the lender's risk is minimized and that the collateral adequately covers the loan amount. Be prepared to provide updated financial information if requested.

Required Documentation for Closing

1. **Loan Agreement and Commitment Letter**

Ensure you have the original signed copies and necessary duplicates of the loan agreement and commitment letter. These documents are the foundation of your loan transaction and must be accurate and complete.

2. **Proof of Collateral and Insurance**
    - **Collateral Documentation:** Provide proof of ownership, such as titles or deeds, for any assets being used as collateral. Ensure that these documents are up-to-date and accurately reflect the value and condition of the collateral.
    - **Insurance Proof:** Demonstrate that you have sufficient insurance coverage on the collateral. This protects both you and the lender against potential losses. The insurance policy should name the lender as the loss payee.

3. **Business Licenses and Legal Documents**

Depending on the type of business, you may need to submit various licenses and legal documents, such as:
    - **Business License:** Verifies that your business is legally registered and authorized to operate.
    - **Articles of Incorporation:** If applicable, these documents establish your business as a legal entity.
    - **Partnership Agreements:** For partnerships, provide the legal agreements that outline the roles and responsibilities of each partner.
    - **Operating Agreements:** For LLCs, provide the operating agreement that governs the management of the company.

4. **Personal Guarantees and Financial Statements**

- **Personal Guarantees:** Often, lenders require personal guarantees from the business owners or key stakeholders. This means that you personally guarantee the repayment of the loan, which reduces the lender's risk.
- **Financial Statements:** Provide the latest financial statements, including:
  - **Balance Sheets:** Reflecting the financial position of your business at a specific point in time.
  - **Income Statements:** Showing the profitability over a specific period.
  - **Cash Flow Statements:** Detailing the inflows and outflows of cash within your business.
  - **Tax Returns:** Recent tax returns may also be required to verify income and financial health.

Tips for a Smooth Closing

1. **Review All Documents Carefully**

Before signing any document, take the time to read it thoroughly. Ensure that all details are correct and that you understand the terms. Pay particular attention to:

- **Interest Rates:** Ensure the rates are as agreed upon.
- **Repayment Terms:** Verify the repayment schedule and due dates.
- **Fees and Charges:** Be aware of any fees, charges, or penalties.
- **Special Conditions:** Ensure any covenants or special conditions are clearly understood.

2. **Ensure All Required Documentation is Complete and Accurate**

Double-check that you have all the necessary documents and that they are accurate and complete. Incomplete or incorrect documentation can cause delays and might even result in the loan being declined at the last minute.

3. **Communicate with Your Lender**

Maintain open and proactive communication with your lender. If you have any questions or concerns, address them promptly. Clear communication helps prevent misunderstandings and ensures that both parties are aligned throughout the closing process.

- **Regular Updates:** Provide your lender with regular updates on any changes in your financial situation.

- **Clarify Doubts:** If there are any terms or clauses you do not understand, ask for clarification.
- **Be Proactive:** Address any potential issues or missing documents as soon as possible to avoid delays.

By following these guidelines and ensuring that you are well-prepared, you can navigate the loan closing process with confidence. This preparation helps ensure that all requirements are met and that you are fully ready to finalize your loan agreement, paving the way for the successful funding of your business needs.

Chapter 10: Managing Your SBA Loan

Making Payments and Managing Loan Terms

Set Up a Payment Schedule to Ensure Timely Payments

Setting up a payment schedule is the first and most crucial step in managing your SBA loan effectively. Here's how to do it in detail:

1. **Identify Your Payment Due Dates**: Begin by thoroughly reviewing your loan agreement to note down the specific due dates for each payment. Typically, SBA loans have monthly payment schedules, but it's essential to confirm the exact dates.

2. **Set Up Calendar Reminders**: Use digital tools like Google Calendar, Outlook, or any other preferred scheduling app to set reminders a few days before and on the due date. This ensures you don't miss any payments.

3. **Automate Payments**: Most banks offer the option to set up automatic payments. Enroll in this service to have the monthly payment automatically deducted from your bank account. Ensure you have sufficient funds in your account to avoid overdraft fees.

4. **Track Your Payments**: Maintain a record of each payment made. This can be in the form of a simple spreadsheet or using financial management software. Tracking helps in reconciling your bank statements and ensures all payments are recorded.

5. **Review Regularly**: Periodically review your payment schedule and records to ensure everything is in order. Adjust your budget if necessary to prioritize loan payments.

Monitor Your Loan Terms and Compliance Requirements

Monitoring your loan terms and compliance requirements involves:

1. **Understanding Loan Terms**: Familiarize yourself with key components such as the interest rate, repayment schedule, and any specific covenants or conditions. This knowledge is crucial for proper loan management.

2. **Compliance Requirements**: SBA loans often come with specific compliance requirements, such as maintaining certain financial ratios or restrictions on additional borrowing. Review these regularly to ensure you remain compliant.

3. **Regular Reviews**: Schedule regular reviews of your loan terms and compliance requirements. Set aside time every quarter to revisit your loan agreement and assess your compliance status.

4. **Documentation**: Keep all loan-related documents organized and easily accessible. This includes the original loan agreement, correspondence with your lender, and records of payments made.

5. **Stay Informed**: Be proactive in understanding any changes in SBA regulations or policies that might affect your loan. Subscribe to updates from the SBA or consult with your lender periodically.

Communicate with Your Lender if You Encounter Any Issues

Effective communication with your lender can help mitigate issues before they escalate:

1. **Immediate Contact**: If you anticipate missing a payment or face financial difficulties, contact your lender immediately. Early communication demonstrates responsibility and can lead to more favorable solutions.
2. **Prepare Information**: When contacting your lender, be prepared with all relevant information. This includes details about your financial situation, reasons for the difficulty, and any documentation that supports your case.
3. **Propose Solutions**: Show initiative by proposing potential solutions such as modified payment schedules or temporary payment reductions. Being proactive can lead to better outcomes.
4. **Follow Up**: After your initial contact, ensure you follow up regularly. Maintain open lines of communication until a resolution is reached and documented.
5. **Professional Demeanor**: Maintain a professional and courteous demeanor in all interactions. Building a positive relationship with your lender can be beneficial in the long run.

Strategies for Loan Repayment

Prioritize Loan Payments to Avoid Late Fees and Penalties

Prioritizing your SBA loan payments is essential to maintain your financial health:

1. **Budget Allocation**: Allocate funds for your loan payments at the beginning of each month. Treat these payments as non-negotiable expenses similar to rent or utilities.
2. **Emergency Fund**: Establish an emergency fund specifically for loan payments. This fund can provide a buffer in case of unexpected financial shortfalls.
3. **Expense Management**: Review and manage your expenses to ensure sufficient funds are available for loan payments. Cut unnecessary costs and focus on essential expenditures.
4. **Cash Flow Analysis**: Regularly analyze your cash flow to anticipate any potential issues. Ensure that inflows are timed to meet your payment schedules.
5. **Late Fee Avoidance**: Understand the penalties associated with late payments. Knowing the financial impact can motivate you to prioritize timely payments.

Consider Refinancing or Restructuring Your Loan if Necessary

Refinancing or restructuring your loan can be a viable strategy in certain situations:

1. **Evaluate Current Terms**: Compare your current loan terms with prevailing market conditions. If interest rates have dropped or your financial situation has improved, refinancing might offer better terms.

2. **Consult Your Lender**: Discuss refinancing or restructuring options with your lender. They can provide insights into available programs or alternative loan structures.

3. **Cost-Benefit Analysis**: Conduct a thorough cost-benefit analysis to understand the financial implications of refinancing or restructuring. Consider factors such as fees, interest rates, and the total cost of the loan over its term.

4. **Professional Advice**: Seek advice from a financial advisor to determine the best course of action. An advisor can provide an objective assessment of your situation and recommend the most beneficial strategy.

5. **Application Process**: If you decide to refinance or restructure, prepare for the application process. Gather necessary documents, such as financial statements, tax returns, and a business plan.

Use Cash Flow Management Techniques to Ensure Adequate Funds for Repayment

Effective cash flow management ensures you have adequate funds to meet your loan obligations:

1. **Forecasting**: Develop detailed cash flow forecasts to predict future inflows and outflows. Use historical data and market trends to create accurate projections.

2. **Invoicing and Receivables**: Implement efficient invoicing practices to ensure timely payments from customers. Follow up on overdue accounts to maintain steady cash inflows.

3. **Expense Control**: Monitor and control your expenses rigorously. Identify areas where costs can be reduced without impacting your operations.

4. **Inventory Management**: Optimize your inventory levels to balance supply with demand. Excess inventory ties up cash that could be used for loan repayment.

5. **Short-Term Financing**: Consider short-term financing options, such as a line of credit, to manage temporary cash shortfalls. Ensure that any short-term borrowing aligns with your overall financial strategy.

What to Do If You Encounter Financial Difficulties

Contact Your Lender Immediately to Discuss Your Situation

Promptly addressing financial difficulties with your lender can lead to positive outcomes:

1. **Immediate Action**: Contact your lender as soon as you recognize potential financial difficulties. Delaying the conversation can worsen the situation.
2. **Detailed Explanation**: Provide a detailed explanation of your circumstances. Include information about your financial position, reasons for the difficulties, and any steps you are taking to improve the situation.
3. **Proposed Solutions**: Offer potential solutions or adjustments to your loan terms. This shows initiative and a willingness to resolve the issue collaboratively.
4. **Documentation**: Prepare and share relevant documentation, such as financial statements, cash flow projections, and any supporting evidence of your financial difficulties.
5. **Follow Through**: Ensure that you follow through on any agreements made with your lender. Maintain open communication until a resolution is reached.

Explore Options Such as Deferment, Forbearance, or Loan Modification

Understanding and utilizing available options can provide relief during tough times:

1. **Deferment**: This option allows you to temporarily postpone loan payments. Typically, deferment is granted under specific conditions, such as economic hardship. Review the eligibility criteria and implications on interest accrual.
2. **Forbearance**: Forbearance permits you to reduce or suspend payments for a specified period. It's a short-term solution that provides breathing room while you address financial challenges. Understand the terms and any additional costs associated.
3. **Loan Modification**: A loan modification permanently alters the terms of your loan. This could involve extending the repayment period, reducing the interest rate, or changing the payment structure. Work with your lender to explore this option if it provides long-term benefits.
4. **Eligibility and Application**: Determine your eligibility for these options and prepare for the application process. This may involve submitting detailed financial information and explaining your situation to your lender.
5. **Impact on Credit**: Be aware of how deferment, forbearance, or modification might impact your credit score and overall financial health. Discuss these implications with your lender and financial advisor.

Seek Advice from a Financial Advisor or SBA Counselor

Professional guidance can help you navigate complex financial situations:

1. **Financial Advisor**: Consult a financial advisor for personalized advice on managing your loan and overall financial health. Advisors can provide strategic insights and help you develop a comprehensive financial plan.

2. **SBA Counselor**: Take advantage of the resources provided by the SBA, including counseling and training services. SBA counselors can offer specific advice on managing your SBA loan and provide support for your business operations.

3. **Professional Network**: Engage with your professional network, including accountants, attorneys, and industry peers. Their experiences and insights can provide valuable perspectives on managing financial difficulties.

4. **Education and Training**: Invest in education and training to improve your financial management skills. Attend workshops, webinars, and courses on topics such as cash flow management, financial planning, and loan management.

5. **Support Systems**: Build a support system that includes both professional advisors and personal mentors. Having a strong network can provide emotional and practical support during challenging times.

By following these detailed guidelines, you can effectively manage your SBA loan, prioritize repayments, and navigate financial difficulties. Consistent communication with your lender, proactive financial management, and seeking professional advice are key to maintaining a healthy loan status and achieving long-term business success.

Chapter 11: SBA Loan Resources and Assistance

Navigating the process of securing a Small Business Administration (SBA) loan can be complex, but there are numerous resources and forms of assistance available to help you succeed. This chapter will explore the various tools and support systems provided by the SBA to ensure you have everything you need to obtain and manage your SBA loan effectively.

Additional SBA Resources

The SBA offers a wealth of resources designed to assist small business owners at every stage of the loan process. These resources are accessible through various channels and provide valuable information and tools to guide you through your business journey.

1. SBA.gov Website

The SBA's official website, SBA.gov, is a comprehensive resource hub for small business owners. It offers detailed information about different types of SBA loans, eligibility criteria, and application processes. Additionally, the website features tools to help you understand the benefits of SBA loans and how to apply for them.

Key Features:

- Detailed guides on SBA loan programs.
- Information on eligibility requirements.
- Step-by-step application instructions.
- Access to forms and documents needed for loan applications.

2. SBA Regional and District Offices

SBA regional and district offices are spread across the United States to provide localized support to small business owners. These offices offer personalized assistance, including help with loan applications, business planning, and accessing other SBA services.

Services Provided:

- One-on-one counseling sessions.
- Workshops and training programs.
- Assistance with SBA loan applications.
- Guidance on SBA loan requirements and eligibility.

3. SBA Learning Center

The SBA Learning Center is an online platform offering a variety of training and educational resources. It provides webinars, courses, and tutorials on topics such as business planning, financial management, and marketing. These resources are designed to help you develop the skills needed to grow your business and successfully navigate the loan application process.

Available Resources:

- Free online courses and tutorials.
- Webinars on business-related topics.
- Interactive learning modules.
- Downloadable guides and templates.

SBA Loan Counseling and Support

In addition to the resources available through SBA platforms, several organizations offer counseling and support services to help you understand and apply for SBA loans. These organizations provide free or low-cost assistance to small business owners.

1. SCORE Mentors

SCORE is a nonprofit organization that provides free business counseling and mentorship to small business owners. With a network of experienced business professionals, SCORE mentors offer personalized advice and support tailored to your specific needs.

How SCORE Can Help:

- Free one-on-one business counseling.
- Mentorship from experienced business professionals.
- Workshops and seminars on business-related topics.
- Assistance with business planning and loan applications.

2. Small Business Development Centers (SBDCs)

SBDCs offer personalized assistance to small business owners through a nationwide network of centers. These centers provide a range of services, including business consulting, training, and access to funding opportunities. SBDCs are a valuable resource for detailed, localized support.

Services Provided:

- Business consulting and coaching.
- Training programs and workshops.
- Help with business plan development.
- Assistance with loan applications and financial projections.

3. Women's Business Centers (WBCs)

WBCs are designed to assist women entrepreneurs by providing resources and support tailored to their unique needs. These centers offer a variety of services, including business counseling, training, and access to funding opportunities.

Services Provided:

- Business counseling and mentorship.
- Training programs and workshops.
- Resources for business planning and growth.
- Assistance with SBA loan applications.

Online Tools and Calculators

The SBA provides several online tools and calculators to help you estimate loan payments, develop business plans, and prepare financial projections. These tools are designed to simplify the process of applying for and managing an SBA loan.

1. SBA Loan Calculators

SBA loan calculators are essential tools for estimating your loan payments and understanding the terms of different loan options. These calculators allow you to input various loan amounts, interest rates, and repayment periods to see how they affect your monthly payments and overall loan cost.

Benefits:

- Estimate monthly loan payments.
- Compare different loan options.
- Plan your budget and cash flow.

2. Business Plan and Financial Projection Templates

Developing a solid business plan and accurate financial projections is crucial for securing an SBA loan. The SBA offers downloadable templates to help you create detailed business plans and financial projections, ensuring you present a compelling case to lenders.

Features:

- Step-by-step business plan templates.
- Financial projection worksheets.
- Sample business plans for reference.

3. SBA Application Checklists and Guides

To ensure you have all the necessary documents and information for your SBA loan application, the SBA provides comprehensive checklists and guides. These resources outline the steps you need to take and the documents you need to gather, making the application process more straightforward and less stressful.

Included Checklists and Guides:

- SBA loan application checklist.
- Guides on preparing financial statements.
- Tips for writing a compelling business plan.

By leveraging these SBA resources and assistance options, you can confidently navigate the SBA loan process and secure the funding you need to grow your business. Whether you need detailed information, personalized support, or practical tools, the SBA and its partners are here to help you succeed.

Chapter 12: Common FAQs

Answers to Frequently Asked Questions about SBA Loans

What types of businesses are eligible for SBA loans?

SBA loans are designed to support small businesses across a wide range of industries. To qualify, a business must meet the following criteria:

1. **Size Standards**: The business must be considered small by SBA standards, which vary by industry. Typically, this includes businesses with up to 500 employees or revenue limits defined by the SBA.

2. **Type of Business**: Most types of for-profit businesses are eligible, including sole proprietorships, partnerships, corporations, and limited liability companies (LLCs). However, certain businesses like those engaged in illegal activities, gambling, or speculative businesses are not eligible.

3. **Location**: The business must operate within the United States or its territories.

4. **Character and Creditworthiness**: The owners must demonstrate good character and a sound credit history.

5. **Ability to Repay**: The business must show that it can repay the loan from its earnings.

How long does the SBA loan application process take?

The timeline for SBA loan processing can vary, but here's a general breakdown:

1. **Preparation**: Collecting all necessary documents and completing the application can take 1-2 weeks.

2. **Submission to the Lender**: Once submitted, the lender's review and decision-making process can take 1-3 weeks.

3. **SBA Review**: After the lender approves the loan, the SBA review and approval process can take an additional 1-2 weeks.

4. **Disbursement**: After SBA approval, loan closing and fund disbursement usually take 1-2 weeks.

Overall, expect the process to take anywhere from 4 to 8 weeks from start to finish.

What are the interest rates and fees for SBA loans?

Interest rates and fees for SBA loans are designed to be affordable for small businesses:

1. **Interest Rates**: The interest rates for SBA loans are generally lower than those for traditional business loans and are tied to the Prime Rate. For example, for the SBA 7(a)

loan, the rates typically range from 2.25% to 4.75% above the Prime Rate, depending on the loan amount and repayment term.

2. **Fees**: Common fees include:
   - **Guarantee Fee**: This fee is a percentage of the loan amount, paid to the SBA to guarantee a portion of the loan. It can range from 0.25% to 3.75%, depending on the loan size.
   - **Servicing Fees**: Annual service fees are also charged by the SBA to the lender and are generally passed on to the borrower.
   - **Other Fees**: These may include packaging fees, closing costs, and third-party fees (such as for appraisals or environmental assessments).

Can I apply for more than one SBA loan?

Yes, businesses can apply for and receive more than one SBA loan, provided they meet the eligibility criteria for each loan and have the capacity to repay multiple loans. Each application will be reviewed on its own merits, and the combined total of all SBA loans must still comply with the SBA's lending limits.

Troubleshooting Common Issues

How to handle a loan denial or delay

If your SBA loan application is denied or delayed, here are steps to take:

1. **Understand the Reason**: Request detailed feedback from the lender to understand why the application was denied or delayed.
2. **Address the Issues**: Work on improving the areas identified. This might include improving your credit score, increasing business revenue, or providing additional documentation.
3. **Reapply or Appeal**: Consider reapplying with a stronger application or appealing the decision if you believe there was a misunderstanding.
4. **Seek Alternative Financing**: Explore other financing options such as microloans, alternative lenders, or crowdfunding platforms.

Tips for improving your application

To enhance your chances of approval:

1. **Strong Business Plan**: Ensure your business plan is thorough, including financial projections, market analysis, and a clear explanation of how the loan will be used.

2. **Financial Health**: Maintain clean and accurate financial records. Show consistent revenue growth and profitability.

3. **Creditworthiness**: Personal and business credit scores should be as high as possible. Address any issues or discrepancies in your credit report.

4. **Collateral**: Offering collateral can strengthen your application and provide the lender with added security.

5. **Professional Guidance**: Consider working with a business advisor or SBA-approved lender who can guide you through the process.

Where to find additional help and resources

Numerous resources are available to assist you with the SBA loan process:

1. **SBA District Offices**: Local SBA offices can provide guidance and support. Find your nearest office on the SBA website.

2. **SCORE**: A nonprofit association offering free, expert advice from volunteer business mentors.

3. **Small Business Development Centers (SBDCs)**: Provide free business consulting and training services.

4. **Women's Business Centers (WBCs)**: Focus on helping women entrepreneurs with business training and counseling.

5. **Online Resources**: The SBA website offers extensive resources, including loan program details, application checklists, and educational materials.

Conclusion

Securing an SBA loan can be a game-changer for your business, providing the capital needed for growth and stability. By understanding the eligibility requirements, preparing a thorough application, and knowing how to troubleshoot common issues, you can navigate the process with confidence. Utilize the available resources to bolster your application and increase your chances of success. Remember, persistence and preparation are key to unlocking the financial support your business needs to thrive.

www.ingramcontent.com/pod-product-compliance
Lightning Source LLC
Chambersburg PA
CBHW071843210526
45479CB00001B/271